STOP PETTING MY PEEVES.

CW00688069

DEATH BEFORE DECAF.

IN MY DEFENSE, I WAS LEFT UNSUPERVISED.

MY BUCKET LIST IS SHORTER
THAN MY F*CK IT LIST.

IF NOT NOW,
HOW ABOUT
NEVER?

SORRY I'M LATE,
I JUST DIDN'T WANT TO COME.

I DON'T CARE ABOUT YOUR KIDS
UNLESS THEY'RE SELLING THIN MINTS.

PATIENCE – FOR WHEN THERE ARE TOO MANY WITNESSES

I COULD REALLY GO FOR A GLASS OF WINE AND A MILLION DOLLARS.

IT'S NEVER TOO LATE TO GO BACK TO BED.

HARD
PASS.

IF IGNORANCE IS BLISS, WHY ARE PEOPLE SO UNHAPPY?

NO TUNA ZONE

YOU! OUT OF THE GENE POOL!

SHOOT FOR THE MOON.
EVEN IF YOU MISS IT YOU'LL LAND IN THE
VAST, COLD, DARK EMPTINESS OF SPACE.

WHY HAVE AMBITION
WHEN YOU CAN JUST LOWER THE BAR?

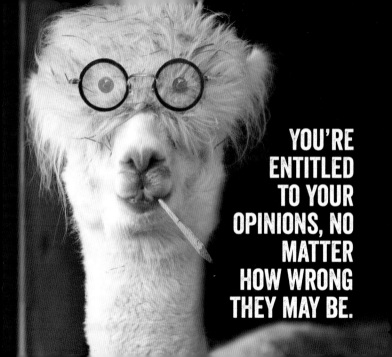

CONFIDENCE:
THE FEELING YOU HAVE BEFORE YOU UNDERSTAND THE SITUATION.

ANYTHING
IS POSSIBLE
FOR THOSE
WHO DON'T
HAVE TO
DO IT.

THE SECRET TO CREATIVITY IS KNOWING HOW TO HIDE YOUR SOURCES.

SOMEBODY HAS TO COME IN LAST.

FAIL HARDER.

THE
RAT RACE
IS OVER.
THE RATS
WON.

DREAM SMALL.

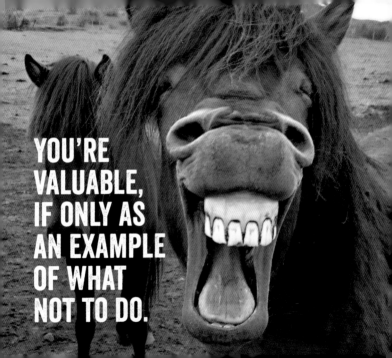

YOU'RE VALUABLE, IF ONLY AS AN EXAMPLE OF WHAT NOT TO DO.

REALITY IS OVERRATED.

TEAMWORK MEANS GETTING ALL THE BLAME FOR EVERYONE'S MISTAKES.

WHAT WOULD SCOOBY DO?

YOU ARE
UNIQUE, JUST
LIKE EVERYONE
ELSE.